Scottish Poems

John Rice was born in Glasgow and spent his childhood in Saltcoats, Ayrshire. For over thirty years he has followed a career as a poet, children's writer, editor, storyteller, performer and photographer, having published books for children, edited a wide selection of arts and literary magazines and anthologies, as well as having written extensively for adults. As a performance poet and storyteller he has appeared at the Edinburgh Festival, the South Bank Centre, the Barbican, Cheltenham Literature Festival and at many arts and book festivals all over the UK. He has read to audiences, young and old, at over 1,500 schools, libraries, arts centres and community venues and been deeply involved in writing competitions and the educational side of contemporary writing.

John Rice has published six books for children (including one of the best-selling children's poetry books of the 1990s, *Bears Don't Like Bananas*, as well as *Dreaming of Dinosaurs*, both illustrated by the acclaimed artist Charles Fuge). He has published six collections of poetry for adults, his most recent being *The Dream of Night Fishers: Scottish Islands in Poems & Photographs*, Scottish Cultural Press.

His poems have appeared in over 150

anthologies, as well as newspapers, magazines and educational books. His broadcast credits include scripts, poetry and stories for BBC television (including the children's programmes *Jackanory*, *English Express* and *A Bear Behind*), the Radio 2 arts programme, Radio 3's poetry and writing programmes and a specially commissioned programme *Into the Fifth Continent* about the Romney Marsh in Kent for Radio 4. In the mid-nineties a short film about him was broadcast by Channel 4 and shown throughout the world.

John Rice is married with two sons and a daughter.

Also available from Macmillan

Irish Poems
Chosen by Matthew Sweeney

Poems of Childhood
Chosen by Brian Moses

The Very Best of Anon.
Poems chosen by John Foster

The Language of Love
Poems chosen by Anne Harvey

Don't Panic!
Poems chosen by Fiona Waters

Scottish Poems

Edited by John Rice

MACMILLAN CHILDREN'S BOOKS

For my nieces and nephews in Ayrshire: Garry & Kaiyliegh Rice, John, Christopher & Zarah Rice, Pamela, Donna, Laura, Steven, Alana & Megan Black, Rebecca Black, Nike & Owen Johnston, Ross & Niaomi Hamilton.

First published 2001 by Macmillan Children's Books

This edition published 2007 by Macmillan Children's Books
a division of Macmillan Publishers Limited
20 New Wharf Road, London N1 9RR
Basingstoke and Oxford
www.panmacmillan.com

Associated companies throughout the world

ISBN: 978-0-330-44059-2

1 3 5 7 9 8 6 4 2

A CIP catalogue record for this book is available from
the British Library.

Printed and bound in China

Acknowledgements

The editor expresses his thanks to the following
people and organizations for their help, support and
encouragement during the editing of this anthology:

The Poetry Library, South Bank, London;
The Scottish Poetry Library, Edinburgh; the staff
of Kent Arts & Libraries, in particular Rick Baker
of Cranbrook Library. A special thank you to
Stewart Conn for his guidance and the
generous gift of his time.

Contents

Land and Sky

Islands and Hinterlands

Animals and Nature

The Magic of an Otherworld

Songs and Sadness

People, Places

Yesterday, Today and Tomorrow

Introduction

I don't often go visiting. That's why each of the poems, lyrics, ballads, riddles, rhymes, catches and mak'-ye-ups contained in this anthology had to come to my door (someone started a rumour about me having a great big clootie dumpling to share). Some banged loudly, some rang the bell fiercely, others knocked gingerly, some tapped. They're all in here, in this house of an anthology, because I believe they are likely to become good friends, and good friends stay around for a lifetime, sometimes longer.

Regarding the poems I sent away; well that was simply because the anthology house is only so big. Many of them were friendly, exceptionally well dressed, spoke like angels and brought nice presents. However, they said they could only stay for the first course and would have to leave straight after.

Of the poems that are now in the anthology house – and it really doesn't matter what age a poem is because they keep themselves fit – I'll say this: they are bright as torches loaded with fresh batteries shining into an unlit room. They aim a beam of light on the joys and celebrations of life, on its secrets, on its difficulties, on its hidden terrors. Poems don't light up the whole room in the way the main light would because they tend to have a much more sharply focused beam. Yet however powerful and instructive they may be, poems do have limits. For example, they can't present us with solutions for the conundrums they point to, nor can they offer remedies to the questions they pose. Poems simply show, they don't ever tell.

When I started work on this anthology I knew that the pieces I chose would inevitably reflect my own values and place on display my own particular tastes in literature. As a poet and storyteller who has specialized in both the publication and performance of my work, I see great similarities between the catching of a poem and the construction of a story. I relate to poetry that has the power to be at once intricate yet understandable, direct yet intriguing, obvious without ever forsaking its innate sense of mystery. Thankfully for us a great deal of Scottish poetry boasts each of these admirable characteristics because, consciously or not, much use is made of the techniques of storytelling in Scottish poetry. The ballads and their enduring song-tales are the most obvious examples.

Then there's song. The Scots tradition plays a vital part in ensuring that song lyrics are seen as the twin brother or sister of poetry. And where there are song lyrics, there are rhythms and rhymes, dances and chimes. An anthology of Scottish poetry would not be complete without songs and tunes tapping their feet, counting the beat – jings, whit a treat!

Perhaps the most important aspect of this book is that you will find fine poets who speak to us in Scotland's three languages – Scots, Gaelic and English. There are poems written in powerful regional speech patterns such as the Shetland and Glasgow dialects, and poems that make full use of colourful local accents. All of these ways of saying have one thing in common, they chime with the unique cultural register of the beginning of the twenty-first century in Britain – that each of these languages, dialects and accents must be treated as equal partners and be valued and prized by all.

I hope you'll stay in the anthology house for a long time – and whether you eat the clootie dumpling all to yourself in one sitting, or just nibble occasionally sharing the feast with friends, well that's fine, just fine.

John Rice
Summer 2001

Water and Weather

Geese tae the sea, guid weather tae be;
Geese tae the hull, guid weather tae spill.

weather rhyme from Angus

November Night, Edinburgh

The night tinkles like ice in glasses.
Leaves are glued to the pavements with frost.
The brown air fumes at the shop windows,
Tries the doors, and sidles past.

I gulp down winter raw. The heady
Darkness swirls with tenements.
In a brown fuzz of cottonwool
Lamps fade up crags, die into pits.

Frost in my lungs is harsh as leaves
Scraped up on paths. – I look up, there,
A high roof sails, at the mast-head
Fluttering a grey and ragged star.

The world's a bear shrugged in his den.
It's snug and close in the snoring night.
And outside like chrysanthemums
The fog unfolds its bitter scent.

Norman MacCaig

Scotland's Winter

Now the ice lays its smooth claws on the sill,
The sun looks from the hill
Helmed in his winter casket,
And sweeps his arctic sword across the sky.
The water at the mill
Sounds more hoarse and dull.
The miller's daughter walking by
With frozen fingers soldered to her basket
Seems to be knocking
Upon a hundred leagues of floor
With her light heels, and mocking
Percy and Douglas dead,
And Bruce on his burial bed,
Where he lies white as may
With wars and leprosy,
And all the kings before
This land was kingless,
And all the singers before
This land was songless,
This land that with its dead and living waits the
    Judgement Day.
But they, the powerless dead,
Listening can hear no more
Than a hard tapping on the sounding floor

A little overhead
Of common heels that do not know
Whence they come or where they go
And are content
With their poor frozen life and shallow banishment.

Edwin Muir

Where Go the Boats?

Dark brown is the river,
    Golden is the sand.
It flows along for ever,
    With trees on either hand.

Green leaves a-floating,
    Castles of the foam,
Boats of mine a-boating –
    Where will all come home?

On goes the river
    And out past the mill,
Away down the valley,
    Away down the hill.

Away down the river,
    A hundred miles or more,
Other little children
    Shall bring my boats ashore.

Robert Louis Stevenson

River, River

River, river,
will you tell me stories?
What did you see on your travels today?

'I saw a fawn standing on a hill top,
and I saw a weasel sliding through a wall.

Then I saw dwarfs with a yellow casket,
and I saw a giant fighting with a bull.'

'I believe about the fawn,
I believe about the weasel,
but not about the dwarfs,
and not about the giant.'

'Well, you asked me for a story,
so I gave you one.
And if you don't believe me
find another stream.'

Iain Crichton Smith

Loch

I have my moods
vagary and whim flit across my surface
I am a looking-glass for the sky
a cradle for mountainous shadows
sometimes wind-ruffled
but deep down untroubled.

I tolerate
dabbling in my shallows.
Throw stones and I spit back.
You want to come a little deeper?
BE WARNED. I'll not be held responsible
for what you can't see.

And I'm greedy
guzzling the white gush
gulping up broad slothful waters
which have lost their way
and every mean and measly trickle
that approaches me.

It's not enough
to be just a pretty sight
I want to burst
from this hollowed bed
it constrains me too neatly.
I want a flood.

I've learned to wait
evaporate my substance
little by frittering little
still sometimes I ripple
with the shivering delight
of my existence.

Helen Lamb

A Cormorant in Oils

Imagine a month
Without washing. Lank hair
Matted on your brow. Skin, grey
And pocked, an ox's jowl.

Imagine eating
When every mouthful tastes
Of gall, and swallowing clogs up
Your throat with oil.

Imagine a bird,
Once a pirate in blacks,
Now, a beggar in a clotted sack.
And don't imagine, see it,

Approach it,
Get within six feet of it.
Then, see it try to open plastered
Wings and fly. See it fail,

Hobble into
The sea and dive. Watch it
Surface over twenty feet away, and
Know, its only future is to die.

Gordon Meade

The Carls o' Dysart*

Tune – Hey, ca' through

Up wi' the carls[1] o' Dysart,
    And the lads o' Buckhaven,
And the kimmers[2] o' Largo,
    And the lasses o' Leven.

Chorus: Hey ca' thro'[3], ca' thro',
          For we hae mickle ado[4];
          Hey ca' thro', ca' thro',
          For we hae mickle ado.

We hae tales to tell,
    An' we hae sangs to sing;
We hae pennies to spend,
    And we hae pints to bring.

We'll live a' our days,
  And them that comes behin',
Let them do the like,
  And spend the gear they win[5].

Robert Burns

This song was based on an old Fifeshire boat-song. The lines of the chorus keep time with the fishermen's oars.

1 old men   2 gossips   3 press on   4 much to do   5 the money they earn

We'll Go To Sea No More

Oh blythely shines the bonnie sun
    Upon the Isle of May,
And blythely comes the morning tide
    Into St Andrew's Bay.
Then up, gude-man, the breeze is fair,
    And up, my braw bairns three;
There's gold in yonder bonny boat
    That sails so well the sea!

I've seen the waves as blue as air,
    I've seen them green as grass;
But I never feared their heaving yet,
    From Grangemouth to the Bass.
I've seen the sea as black as pitch,
    I've seen it white as snow:
But I never feared its foaming yet,
    Though the winds blew high or low.

I never liked the landsman's life,
    The earth is aye the same;
Give me the ocean for my dower,
    My vessel for my hame.
Give me the fields that no man ploughs,
    The farm that pays no fee:
Give me the bonny fish that dance
    Aye merrily in the sea!

The sun is up, and round Inchkeith
    The breezes softly blaw;
The gude-man has his lines aboard –
    Awa', my bairns, awa'.
An' ye'll be back by gloaming grey,
    An' bright the fire will low,
An' in your tales and songs we'll tell
    How weel the boat ye row.

Anon.

Land and Sky

'O Caledonia! stern and wild
Meet nurse for a poetic child!'

Sir Walter Scott (1771–1832)

Oh, Wert Thou in the Cauld Blast

Oh, wert thou in the cauld blast,
   On yonder lea, on yonder lea,
My plaidie to the angry airt[1],
   I'd shelter thee, I'd shelter thee:
Or did Misfortune's bitter storms
   Around thee blaw, around thee blaw,
Thy bield[2] should be my bosom,
   To share it a', to share it a'.

Or were I in the wildest waste
   Sae black and bare, sae black and bare,
The desert were a paradise,
   If thou wert there, if thou wert there;
Or were I monarch o' the globe,
   Wi' thee to reign, wi' thee to reign;
The brightest jewel in my crown
   Wad[3] be my queen, wad be my queen.

Robert Burns

1 quarter   2 shelter   3 would

The Coming of Spring

The brattle o stanes[1] that heralds avalanche
As souchan[2] trees wind-whisper the breiran[3] storm
Sae felt I in the bluid[4] a fluther[5] o wings

The drum and pipe o Pan and his ramstougerous[6] rout
I heard the far fell cry o Aphrodite's horn
And snuff't[7] the rank bouquet o luve's approach.

Sydney Goodsir Smith

1 loud clatter   2 sighing   3 brewing   4 blood   5 flutter   6 boisterous   7 sniffed

The Lee-Rigg

Will ye gang o'er the lee-rigg[1],
    My ain[2] kind deary O!
And cuddle there sae kindly
    Wi' me, my kind deary O?

At thornie-dike[3] and birken-tree[4]
    We'll daff[5], and ne'er be weary O;
They'll scug ill[6] een[7] frae you and me,
    Mine ain kind deary O.

Nae herds[8] wi' kent[9] or colly there,
    Shall ever come to fear ye O;
But lav'rocks[10], whistling in the air,
    Shall woo, like me, their deary O!

While others herd their lambs and ewes,
    And toil for warld's gear[11], my jo[12],
Upon the lee my pleasure grows,
    Wi' you, my kind deary O!

Robert Fergusson

---

1 meadow ridge   2 own   3 hawthorn hedge   4 birch   5 dally   6 screen all   7 eyes
8 shepherds   9 pole for leaping ditches   10 larks   11 worldly riches   12 sweetheart

Dancing Skies

Today is the day of the Dancing Sky
When clouds are thrilled in quadrilles
And swallows are ariel
Masters of lithesome eightsome reels.

Where the aspen giggles and shivers,
Playing the blushing virgin
In a clutter of delicate leaves,
Her petticoats ruffled but clean.

Today is the day of the high wind coming
Mackereled and horsemaned and torn,
Ripped into shapes and spat onto blue
Waiting for an adventure to be born.

The crackling burn by the broken bridge
Rises and floods with a galloping roar
To the surfing ducks who splutter and splash
From raging stream to the rocky shore.

Today is the day of the grey heron rising
On thermals and updrafts
With spirits soaring
To reach the gods and doff a cap

to heaven.

Siùsaidh NicNèill

Making Hay

Cutting grass, I used to drive Dad
Wild. He would align me with the topmost
Tree and at my crazy zig-zag
Smash his hand against his brow
And say it was deliberate.

Truth is, I loved to leave
Substantial lines of Indian
Scalp two feet or so apart.
Today, a small boy smiles up
At me, his tiny bike abandoned
By our neat parterre, listening
In glee to enraged dog turd
Whip around the blades.

Now I get it straight
For all the 'neighbours'
Who come from round the block
Just to watch us cut the grass:
Me mowing, him hoeing up the hay.

I smile at them as at the old
Crail lady who used to man
Her garden gate each morning
Just to see me smile,
'A special smile,' she said.

David Kinloch

The Tree

The heart is a tree for love:
And is a flowery tree
When in its shade the dove
Sings and is free.

Make but your heart a cage,
To hold what you desire,
And song is turned to rage;
Blossom to brier.

William Soutar

Blue Bonnets Over the Border

March, march, Ettrick and Teviotdale,
  Why the deil dinna ye march forward in order?
March, march, Eskdale and Liddesdale,
  All the Blue Bonnets are bound for the Border.
      Many a banner spread
      Flutters above your head,
  Many a crest that is famous in story,
      Mount and make ready then,
      Sons of the mountain glen,
Fight for the Queen and the old Scottish glory!

Come from the hills where your hirsels are grazing,
  Come from the glen of the buck and the roe;
Come to the crag where the beacon is blazing,
  Come with the buckler, the lance and the bow.
      Trumpets are sounding,
      War-steeds are bounding,
  Stand to your arms then, and march in good order,
      England shall many a day
      Tell of the bloody fray,
When the Blue Bonnets came over the Border!

Sir Walter Scott

'A Good Sink': An Anecdote

I must tell you this, though.
It's this. That we were up in Sutherland.
Thinking of buying a house.
We'd seen one advertised, but when
we got there it was all shut up.
We looked around outside anyway,
peering through the windows and so on.
A man came up to us. Local.
'Do you want a house to buy?'
he said. 'I've got a house you can buy.'
He insisted, really insisted,
so we followed him. He took us
inside. 'Look,' he said.
'It's got a sink.' (Full of peelings
and filthy dishes.) 'A good sink.'
We nodded, 'A good sink, yes.'
'And a cooker. A good cooker.'
'A good cooker, yes.' 'A good cooker.
It cooks. It works.' Yes. Yes.
We nodded. We knew it could cook
from the pot-pourri glazed on the hob.
'I'll just phone them, then,' he said.
'I'll phone them. You stay there.'

He lifted the receiver, dialled
and waited. A good sink.
A good cooker. This house?
This man? He was speaking.
Pausing. Speaking. Our eyes
trailed the flex to its disconnection
at the socket. 'We need to go now.
Now. Sorry. We're – we're late.
Must go.' 'What? Just a— No, wait.
It's good. It's good. A good sink.
A good—' We backed away.
Later that day, he took a razor
to the minister.

Douglas Lipton

Kite

That's me up there
caught in the wind's claws
held slant to the land
at the end of my string. I'm
a scrap of orange
in a blue bowl
a fingernail scraping thumbed
against the sky and I laugh
for the wind can't tear me,
though I toss from side to side.
People stop by lochs
or come out of their houses
on the flat brown moor
laughing and pointing.

'This is me up here!'
– as the big wind buffets
and gusts –
'Just doing my job.'

And I want to chase after the sky
to swoop down behind those islands
to the blue sea.
But they tug me in.
They play me like a fish.

Then they put me in the garage
with my string wound up beside me.
And I wait.

David Scott

The Berryfields o' Blair

When berry-time comes roond each year, Blair's
  population's swellin',
There's every kind o' picker there and every kind
  o' dwellin';
There's tents and huts and caravans, there's bothies
  and there's bivvies,
Ay, and shelters made wi' tattie-bags and dugouts
  made wi' divvies.

There's traivellers fae the Western Isles, fae Arran,
  Mull and Skye,
Fae Harris, Lewis and Kyles o' Bute they come their
  luck to try;
Fae Inverness and Aberdeen, fae Stornoway and Wick,
A' flock to Blair at the berry-time, the straws and rasps
  to pick.

Noo, there's corner-boys fae Glesca, kettle-boilers fae
  Lochee,
And miners fae the pits o' Fife, mill-workers fae Dundee;
And fisherfolk fae Peterheid, and tramps fae everywhere,
A' lookin' for a livin' aff the berryfields o' Blair.

Noo, there's some wha earn a pound or twa, some
    cannae earn their keep,
And some would pick fae morn to nicht, and some
    would rather sleep;
There's some wha' has to pick or starve and some wha'
    dinnae care,
There's some wha' bless and some wha' curse the
    berryfields o' Blair.

Noo, there's families pickin' for one purse and some
    wha' pick alane,
And there's men wha' share and share alike wi' wives
    that's no' their ain;
There's gladness and there's sadness tae, there's happy
    hairts and sair,
For there's comedy and tragedy played on the fields o'
    Blair.

But afore I've put my pen awa', it's this I would like to
    say:
You'll traivel far afore you'll meet a kinder lot than they;
For I've mixed wi' them in field and pub, and while
    I've breath to spare,
I'll bless the hand that led me to the berryfields o' Blair.

Belle Stewart

The Flowers of the Forest

I've heard the lilting at our yowe[1]-milking
    Lasses a-lilting before the dawn o' day;
But now they are moaning on ilka green loaning[2];
    'The Flowers of the Forest are a' wede[3] away.'

At buchts[4], in the morning, nae blythe lads are scorning;
    The lasses are lonely, and dowie and wae[5];
Nae daffin'[6], nae gabbin'[7], but sighing and sabbing[8]
    Ilk ane lifts her leglen[9], and hies[10] her away.

In hairst[11], at the shearing, nae youths now are jeering,
    The bandsters[12] are lyart[13], and runkled[14] and grey;
At fair or at preaching, nae wooing, nae fleeching[15]:
    The Flowers of the Forest are a' wede away.

At e'en, in the gloaming, nae swankies[16] are roaming
    'Bout stacks wi' the lasses at bogle[17] to play,
But ilk ane sits drearie, lamenting her dearie:
    The Flowers of the Forest are a' wede away.

Dule and wae[18] for the order sent our lads to the Border;
    The English, for ance[19], by guile wan the day;
The Flowers of the Forest, that foucht[20] aye the foremost,
    The prime o' our land are cauld in the clay.

We'll hear nae mair lilting at the yowe-milking,
    Women and bairns are heartless and wae;
Sighing and moaning on ilka green loaning;
    'The Flowers of the Forest are a'wede away.'

Jane Elliot

Note:

The touching melancholy and acute sense of loss encapsulated in these beautiful lyrics commemorate the Battle of Flodden, September, 1513, in which the opposing English and Scottish armies numbered about 20,000 men each. The battlefield became so muddied that some of the Scots cast off their shoes and fought in their hose. However, when it came to close-quarter fighting, the 20-feet long Swiss pikes used by the Scots were no match for the shorter English halberd. The English claimed that up to 10,000 Scots fell. While this figure is disputed, there is no doubt that, for a small and sparsely populated country such as Scotland, the loss of so many men had a devastating effect on the country.

*1 ewe 2 lane 3 withered 4 sheep folds 5 sad and sorrowful 6 dallying
7 chatting 8 sobbing 9 milk-pail 10 hides 11 harvest 12 binders 13 grizzled
14 wrinkled 15 flattering 16 cool dudes 17 peek-a-boo game
18 sorrow and woe 19 for once 20 fought*

Jock, Since Ever I Saw Your Face

Jock, since ever I saw yer face
    Jock, since ever I kent ye
Jock, since ever I saw yer face
    dae ye mind o' the shillin' I lent ye?

Lost ma love an' I dinna ken hoo
    lost ma love an' I care na'
the losin' o' wan's the gainin' o' twa
    I'll find me another I fear na'.

Traditional

My Heart's in the Highlands

Tune – Failte na Miosg

Farewell to the Highlands, farewell to the north,
The birthplace of Valour, the country of Worth;
Wherever I wander, wherever I rove,
The hills of the Highlands for ever I love.

Chorus: My heart's in the Highlands, my heart is not here;
My heart's in the Highlands, a-chasing the deer;
A-chasing the wild-deer and following the roe,
My heart's in the Highlands, wherever I go.

Farewell to the mountains high-cover'd with snow;
Farewell to the straths and green vallies below;
Farewell to the forests and wild-hanging woods;
Farewell to the torrents and loud-pouring floods.

Robert Burns

Islands and Hinterlands

'The cadences that wind and tide are weaving
In Gaelic words.'

from 'Ealasaid' by
Helen B. Cruickshank (1886–1975)

Viking Boy

a sandstorm strips the dune
to bare-bones
on a straw mat
over a bed of feathers
the boy lies
a hoop of metal
shelters his head
the shield over his face
the sword by his flank
he has a bone comb
not a yellow hair in it
the bed to soften
the blow to the boy
the shield to hide
his young face
from the sharp scatter
from the first handful of sand

Valerie Gillies

Gearradh na Mònadh à Smeircleit

Taigh Fhionnlaigh,
Taigh a' Bhaoghlaich,
Taigh Aonghais a' Cheanadaich,
Taigh Aonghais 'ac Dhòmhnaill,
Taigh Alasdair Ruaidh,
Taigh Dhomhachain
Taigh an Ruaidh,
Taigh Dhòmhnaill Eachainn,
Taigh Sheumais Shlàdair,
Taigh Sheòrais
Taigh a' Chlachair,
Taigh Sheonaidh Mhòir,
Taigh Alasdair Dhuibh,
Taigh Phàdraig Eòghainn,
Taigh Sheonaidh Ailein,
Taigh Dhòmhnaill Penny,
Taigh Iagain Dhòmhnaill.
   Mar a bha,
    's mar a tha,
    's mar a bhitheas.
      Fad saoghal nan saoghal.
     Amen.

Angus Peter Campbell

Garrynamonie from Smerclate

Finlay's house,
The Benbecula man's house,
Angus son of the Kennedy's house,
Angus McDonald's house,
Red Alasdair's House,
Domhachann's house,
A Ruaidh's house,
Donald Hector's house,
Seumas Shladair's house,
George's house,
The Stonemason's house,
Big Johnny's house,
Black Alasdair's house,
Patrick Ewen's house,
Seonaidh Allan's house,
Donald son of Penny's house,
Iagan Dhomhnaill's house.
            As it was,
            is,
            and will be.
                World without end.
                Amen.

Angus Peter Campbell

Ròdhag, 2000 A.D.

Nuair a bheir an fheannag
an t-sùil às a' chaora mu dherieadh,
bidh mi ri dìdearachd air d' uinneagan:
bidh iad an sin
a' cluich chairtean
's ag òl Beaujolais,
poodle a' dannsa mun casan;
bidh fhàileadh blàth a' bhainne air falbh as na
bàthchannan,
's iad làn thruinnsearan fuar cruaidh *pottery*
airson an luchd-turais;
fuaim nam brògan tacaideach nan samhla
a' coiseadh air monadh;
na croitean uaine fàsail
gun bhristeadh spaide.

> Nuair a bheir an fheannag
> an t-sùil as a' chaora mu dheireadh,
> bidh mi ri farchluais
> air d' uinneagan,
> rid osagan ag ochanaich,
> 's na guthan cruaidh Sasannach
> a' dol an aghaidh na gaoith.

Catriona NicGumaraid
(Catriona Montgomery)

Roag, 2000 A.D.

When the hoodie crow takes
the eye out of the last sheep
I will be peeping in at your windows.
They will be there,
playing cards,
drinking Beaujolais,
a poodle prancing about their feet.
The warm smell of the milk will have left the byres
and they will be full of hard cold pottery for the tourists;
the sound of tackety boots like ghosts walking on the
    moors,
the crofts green and unproductive
without spade-breaking.

When the hoodie crow takes
the eye out of the last sheep
I will be eavesdropping at your windows
listening to your breezes sighing
and the harsh English voices clashing with the wind.

Catriona NicGumaraid
(Catriona Montgomery)

The Dump, Outside Portree, Isle of Skye

Seagulls,
scavenging for fish or apples or bread,
wheel above broken washing machines and smashed
    mirrors.

There's a child's pram,
all
askew,
with one torn rubber tyre.

A doll without a head,
a spade without a shaft,
a car without a door.

Green filament netting protects the debris from the
    circling crows
mercilessly eyeing a fish-bone beside the headless doll.

And I think of how our inheritance has been dumped
behind the inadequacy of a filament net,
the TV screen of our day.

Angus Peter Campbell

An Incomplete History of
Rock Music in the Hebrides

Peewits quiffed like Elvis reel from rocks,
their sheen of feathers like blue suede
the breeze buffs in the midday air.
'He loves ewe. Meah! Meah! Meah!'
bleat a Fat Four of blackface sheep
beneath mop-tops of unshorn hair.

Jagged stalks of thistles strut,
flashing menace in the evening light
before a group of timeworn stones.
Spangled with glitter, starlings soar
and oystercatchers sport red lips
while herons stalk on platform soles.

Each fulmar packs its pistol.
There's anarchy on cliff-tops
as they reel and spit on rocks below.
Then a riff is played on marram grass,
shells syncopate on shorelines as
night downs its curtain on the show.

Donald S. Murray

Càradh

'S math nach do thilg mi às mo spaid.

Chan eil fiù's spota meirg air
ged a tha e air fàs caran maol
leis na fhuair e de chleachdadh.

Mach leam a-rithist gu mullach an lot
airson toll eile' a chladhach
agus gaol eil' a chàradh
anns an ùir.

Deàgh thodhar dham chuid bhàrdachd
ged a b'fheàrr leam a bhi sàmhach
le mo ghaol nam ghàirdeanan.

Anne C. Frater

Burying

Just as well I kept my spade.

Not a spot of rust on it
although it's a bit blunt
through all the use it's had.

Out again to the top of the croft
to dig another hole
and bury another love
in the ground.

Fertile soil for my poems
although I'd rather be silent
with my love in my arms.

Anne C. Frater

An dèidh an Tòrraidh

Tha a' bhantrach na seasamh aig an doras,
a ceann an taic a' bhalla.
Tha gach rud sàmhach.
Tha na h-aoighean air am biathadh
is a' mhòr-chuid air falbh,
am bàgh 's am baile glas glas,
's na bàtaichean-iasgaich a' gabhail a-mach gun fhuaim.
Cluinnidh i còmhradh nam bana-chàirdean sa chidsin
is na bodaich, len dramannan,
a' bruidhinn air beatha dheagh-bheusach.
'Ann an dòigh 's e latha toilicht' a bh' againn,'
tha i ag ràdh, a' coimhead a cuid mhac,
is aogas athar ann an aodann gach fir dhuibh.

Gu h-obann sàthaidh a' ghrian a-mach
bannan liomaid-bhuidhe
thar nan raon de dh'fhochann gruamach,
is sguabar dràgonan ceathach an-àirde
's air falbh thar a' bhàigh,
is mar a thionndaidheas i a-staigh
chithear fhathast mu h-aodann
gaol an fhir mhairbh air an àit'.

Meg Bateman

After the Funeral

The widow stands at the door
and leans her head against the wall.
All is quiet.
The guests are fed
and mostly gone,
and the sea and the town are grey, grey,
with the fishing boats silently putting out.
She hears the talk of the women in the kitchen
and the old men with their drams
discussing a life well lived.
'It's kind of been a happy day,'
she says, looking at her boys,
each with his something
of his father in his face.

Suddenly the sun stabs out bars
of lemon-yellow light
over the fields of glowering corn,
dragons of mist are whisked up
and away across the bay,
and as she turns back to the house
you can still see in her face
the dead man's love for it all.

Meg Bateman

Island School

A boy leaves a small house
   Of sea light. He leaves
      The sea smells, creel
      And limpet and cod.

The boy walks between steep
   Stone houses, echoing
      Gull cries, the all-around
      Choirs of the sea,

Ship noises, shop noises, clamours
   of bellman and milkcart.
      The boy comes at last
      To a tower with a tall desk

And a globe and a blackboard
   And a stern chalk-
      smelling lady. A bell
      Nods and summons.

A girl comes, cornlight
   In the eyes, smelling
      Of peat and cows
      And the rich midden.

Running she comes, late,
   Reeling in under the last
      Bronze brimmings. She sits
      Among twenty whispers.

George Mackay Brown

Lönabrack[1] at Littlure

Laevin Burrastow, hills winter ochre
we lean inta da wind, alang banks' gaets.
Luckit[2] bi da updraa, maas[3] lift
ta plane in silence.

Drappin doon ta da loch o Quinnigyo
April sun is warm.
A pair o' rain geese[4] mak fur da hill
an a laverock is a ringin string[5]
ta da lunder o ocean bass.

Climbin, we mak da bicht o Littlure;
Foula stepped apo da skyline.
Atlantic rollers brack,
kirn ita gyos,
höv[6] spindrift[7];
black headlands settle
in a böl[8] o' froad,
sharpenin clooers[9].

Back o'er ta Quinnigyo, we crug[10]
lik kittiwakes anunder banks, watch
bowes and corks drift seawirds.
Waves at's birled fae Labrador lirk[11] in;
steer a sheeksin[12] atween shalls an stons.

Doon owre da broo at last ta Burrastow,
wind-hattered but foo o newness.
Da sea kwilks[13] in an oot,
a selkie[14] basks,
an, fur a blink,
he taks wis back
ta wir beginnings.

Christine De Luca

1 surf   2 tempted   3 seagulls   4 red-throated divers   5 traditional Shetland fiddling
involves the playing of two strings simultaneously, creating a resonance.   6 heave
7 sea spray   8 where an animal lies   9 claws   10 crouch   11 crease, wrinkle
12 blethering   13 makes a swallowing sound   14 seal

A Shuttle o' Soonds

The Shetland dialect

At da time at folk namit da nort end o Eden
a moothfoo o soonds gied frame tae da laand
every bicht, every knowe a wird pictir in Norn.

Dey hed böddies[1] o wirds for da varg[2] o da crofter
soonds o da crö[3], da crub[4] an da hill: some lost
on da wind owre da flakki[5] o years.

An a kyist-foo[6] o soonds for aa kinds o sea wark
wi a hoidy-hol[7] for queer luckin wirds[8]
stowed far fae wir hearin ta keep herm awa.

Da Norn[9] is lang gien, but hit's left a waageng[10]
at keetchins a tongue at can hadd ony haert[11]
can rowe up[12] wir feelings, unreffel[13] wir tochts.

For every haand's turn[14] still a mird[15] o wird patterns
lik an allover gansey[16], a wirkin man's sark
med ta be worn, no laid up for best.

We man savour wir words is dey tirl on da tongue
lik snorie-ben[17], sneester[18] and skaddyman's heid[19]
wird laalies[20] fur aabody, no jöst fur bairns.

Fur dey mak da warp in a pattern o livin, while
da weft comes fae places ootbye da Sooth Mooth.[21]
Dey can blend i da waeve wi wir shuttle o soonds.

Da garb o wir language is pitten[22] dagidder[23]
in a wye at maks room fur da new and da auld[24]
baith pipeline an paet-bank; rap artist an skald.

Christine De Luca

1 straw basket for carrying over the shoulder   2 messy work   3 sheep-fold
4 small, circular dry-stone enclosure for plants   5 straw mat over which corn was
winnowed 6 kist-full   7 hiding place   8 enticing   9 a variant of Old Norse spoken
in Shetland until the 17th century   10 aftertaste   11 sustain anyone   12 wrap up
13 untangle   14 a stroke of work   15 swarm, throng   16 jumper with Fair Isle
patterns all over   17 a toy made from bone and string with a twist which makes
a snoring noise   18 a private chuckle   19 sea urchin   20 playthings   21 the south
entrance to Lerwick harbour   22 put   23 together   24 old

Leaving Stromness

always, the salt, the tear:

nestled houses gather distance
solid on the hill, unblinking

till, on the Ness, one handkerchief,
one arm waving.

Anne MacLeod

Animals and Nature

The man who cleans his dish with the cat's tail says
'This is a long way from elegance.'

Gaelic Proverb

Orkney: The Whale Islands

Sharp spindrift struck
At prow's turning.
Then the helmsman,
'Either whales to starboard
Or this storm
Is thrusting us at Thule,
Neighbour to bergs, beneath
The boreal star.'
Sunset. We furled ship
In a wide sea-loch.
Star-harrows
Went over our thin sleep.
Dawn. A rainbow crumbled
Over Orc, 'whale islands'.
Then the skipper, 'The whales
Will yield this folk
Corn and fleeces and honey.'
And the poet,
'Harp of whalebone, shake
Golden words from my mouth.'

George Mackay Brown

The Wren and the Robin

The wren she lies in care's bed[1],
    In care's bed, in care's bed,
The wren she lies in care's bed,
    In mickle dule and pyne[2], O,
When in came Robin Redbreast,
    Redbreast, Redbreast,
When in came Robin Redbreast,
    Wi' succar-saps[3] and wine, O.

Now, maiden, will ye taste o' this,
    Taste o' this, taste o' this,
Now, maiden, will ye taste o' this?
    It's succar-saps and wine, O.
Na, ne'er a drap, Robin,
    Robin, Robin,
Na, ne'er a drap, Robin,
    Gin it was ne'er so fine, O.

And whaur's the ring that I gied ye,
    That I gied ye, that I gied ye,
And whaur's the ring that I gied ye,
    Ye little cutty quyne[4], O?
I gied it till a soger[5],
    A soger, a soger,
I gied it till a soger,
    A kind sweetheart o' mine, O.

Traditional

1 sickbed   2 much sadness and pain   3 sugar sops
4 a folk name for the wren   5 to a soldier

Crabs: Tiree

We tied a worm of bacon fat
to a flat rock with string
and dropped it over the edge
into the clear water
of the bay. It fell gently

to the sand and the seaweed.
A tug told us we'd a bite
or we saw the crab itself
latch onto the ragged fat and pulled it
steadily out: this was the knack.

Too sudden, too sharp
and it dropped from its stone
shadow, so clumsily evading
its fate. But smoothly,
feeding the rough string

through fist upon fist
and they would come to us
like lumps of lava, water
sluicing from their backs.
Dumbly determined
 they hung on

by one improbable claw
before the dull crack as they hit
the harbour wall, or the side
of the pails we kept them in.

Standing in a row,
four or five of us holiday kids
pulled out scores in a day, till each
bucket was a brackish mass
of fearsome crockery

bubbling below
its skin of salt water.
What happened to them all? –
our train of buckets, the great stench
of our summer sport.

It was a blond boy
from Glasgow finally pushed me in,
head over heels, from where
I crouched on the pier wall.
When I righted myself

I was waist-deep in crab-
infested waters. No one
could pull me out. 'You must walk
to the shore,' my sister shouted
as I held my hands

high above my head,
thinking I could at least
save them. But how beautiful
it was all around me! The spatter
of green crofts

and deep blue lochans;
the cottontail; the buttercup
on the cropped foreshore. The sky
was depthless; all was silence.
And I was there

moving slowly through
this perfect blue wedge,
bearing terror in one hand, guilt
in the other, leaving the briefest wake
to mark my shame.

Tom Pow

Snailie

Snailie snailie on the waa,
Are ye niver feart ye'd fa?
Wi yer hoosie on yer back
Like a hiker wi a pack?
Feech, snailie! Dicht yer snoot!
Slivvrin ower the watter spoot!

Sheena Blackhall

The Cat's Tale

The cat doesn't understand
about reading
or the space between
my eyes and the paper
or the stillness.
The silence.

She pops up
between my propped elbows
soft as peach and ashes
under my chin
executes feline twirls
then lodges her tail
below my nose
so I can smell
how clean she is.

She sits on the page
translates the words
into thrumming
cheek-butts my nose
jaggy-licks my eyelid shut
and spins me
a compelling tale
of love beyond words.

Valerie Thornton

One Gone, Eight to Go

On a night of savage frost,
This year, my smallest cat,
The fluffy one, got lost.
And I thought that that was that.

Until, late home, I heard,
As I fumbled for my key,
The weak sound of some bird.
He was there, mewing to me.

There, on the icy sill,
Lifting his crusted head,
He looked far worse than ill.
He looked, I'd say, quite dead.

Indoors, though, he could eat,
As he showed, and fluffed his tail.
So much for a plate of meat.
So much for a storm of hail.

Now, by the burning grate,
I stroke his fragile spine,
Thinking of time, and fate.
Lives go. Men don't have nine,

As kittens do, to waste.
This lucky one survives,
And purrs, affronted-faced.
But even he, who thrives

Tonight, in my cupped hands,
And will grow big and grey,
Will sense, in time, the sands,
And fail, and shrink away.

George MacBeth

The Bubblyjock

It's hauf like a bird and hauf like a bogle[1]
And juist stands in the sun there and bouks[2].
It's a wunder its heid disna burst
The way it's aye raxin' its chouks[3].

Syne it twists its neck like a serpent
But canna get oot a richt note
For the bubblyjock swallowed the bagpipes
And the blether[4] stuck in its throat.

Hugh MacDiarmid

1 scarecrow   2 hiccups   3 stretching its jaws   4 bladder

Three Wee Craws Sat Upon a Wa'

Three wee craws sat upon a wa'
  sat upon a wa', sat upon a wa'.
Three wee craws sat upon a wa'
  on a cold and frosty morning.

The first wee craw couldnae flee at a'
  couldnae flee at a', couldnae flee at a'.
The first wee craw couldnae flee at a'
  on a cold and frosty morning.

The second wee craw wis greetin' fur his maw
  greetin' fur his maw, greetin' fur his maw.
The second wee craw wis greetin' fur his maw
  on a cold and frosty morning.

The third wee craw wisnae there at a'
  wisnae there at a', wisnae there at a'.
The third wee craw wisnae there at a'
  on a cold and frosty morning.

Traditional

Luck

My neighbour has a black cat.
Every day it crosses my garden path
and brings me luck.

Lately I discovered the reason.
It crosses my path to sit under the hedge
and wait for thrushes.

Hidden good luck for me. Bloody bad luck for thrushes.

So today I bought a piece of fish
and placed it exactly

where the cat could cross far enough to bring me luck
but not so far that it need threaten the thrushes.

The cat was delighted.
It crossed my path and brought me luck.
It ate up all the fish

then went to sit under the hedge,

leaving me to ponder my next gesture,
trying to wash the fishy smell off my hands.

Robin Bell

Grey Geese

All night they flew over in skeins.
I heard their wrangling far away
Went out once to look for them, long after midnight.
Saw them silvered by the moonlight, like waves,
Flagging south, jagged and tired,
Across the sleeping farms and the autumn rivers
To the late fields of autumn.

Even in a city I have heard them
Their noise like the rusty wheel of a bicycle;
I have looked up from among the drum of engines
To find them in the sky
A broken arrowhead turning south
Heading for home.

The Iceland summer, the long light
Has run like rivers through their wings,
Strengthened the sinews of their flight
Over the whole ocean, till at last they circle,
Straggle down on the chosen runway of their field.

They come back
To the same place, the same day, without fail;
Precision instruments, a compass
Somewhere deep in their souls.

Kenneth C. Steven

Lìon

Fìnealta, foinnidh,
le snàithleanan mìne
's dealbhadh cuimir,
dlùth-thoinnte sa' mheadhon
's a' sgaoileadh uidh air n-uidh
gu ruig nan oirean,
bannan geomeatraiceach
ga cheangal ri na prìomh thaodan,
's gach snàithlean, bann is taod
a' glacadh faileas na grèine,
na gathan a' ruith 's a' stad
mar a ghluaiseas na h-acraichean duilleach,
gach nì ullamh
mu choinneamh nan cuileag,
obair ghrinn mharbhteach Nàdair,
uaigh is caladh,
foill is tàladh
lìon an damhain-allaidh.

Ruaraidh MacThòmais
(Derick Thomson)

Web

Elegant, shapely,
using fine threads
and neat design,
tightly intertwined at the centre
and stretching little by little
to the edges,
with geometric bonds
connecting with the main cables,
and every cable, bond and thread
catching the sun's sheen,
the rays running and stopping
as the leafy anchors move,
everything ready
for the approach of the flies,
Nature's neat deadly work,
grave and harbour,
deceit and enticement
of the spider's web.

Derick Thomson
(Ruaraidh MacThòmais)

Seal

– Mother, I can hear a baby crying,
Out there in the sea, is it drowning or dying?

– No no, my lamb, that's not what you hear.
It is only a seal, go to sleep, never fear.

– There's another, and another, oh it is so sad.
How can an animal make us feel bad?

– I don't know, my dear, maybe they smell
The fishermen with clubs, fearful and fell.

– Why do they kill them? No wonder they cry.
Do the men never have a tear in their eye?

– Oh no, the seals kill the beautiful fish
That make our supper a beautiful dish.

– And we kill the fish. Everything we kill.
We dig a grave and it's too big to fill!

– Darling, it has to be. We are killed too.
Seventy years and the message comes through.
– Oh mother, the night is so cold and so wild!
Listen, listen, I am sure it is a child!

Edwin Morgan

The Song of the Grasshopper

First of all, it is their songs
That she listens for, the dry chirr
Of thigh against thigh, the dead give-away
As to where they are hiding, serenading
Each other in the knee-high grass.

Bent over double, or on all-fours,
She tracks them down with the diligence
Of bloodhounds, and then, to my amazement,
Pounces, and they are hers. Then, slowly,
She opens her hands and begins to sing.

And the wonder of it is, that they
Stand in her palms and listen. As if her
Song was their reward for her four-year-old
Rough-handling. As her voice trails off,
The grasshoppers become their names,

And disappear.

Gordon Meade

Daddy-Lang-Legs

Daddy-lang-legs like a crane,
Stots against the windae pane.
On his stilts he styters ben,
Wandrin Willies in the fen,
Like a muckle lang giraffe . . .
Ower mony legs bi hauf!

Sheena Blackhall

Midge

The evening is perfect, my sisters.
The loch lies silent, the air is still.
The sun's last rays linger over the water
and there is a faint smirr, almost a smudge
of summer rain. Sisters, I smell supper,
and what is more perfect than supper?
It is emerging from the wood,
in twos and threes, a dozen in all,
making such a chatter and a clatter
as it reaches the rocky shore,
admiring the arrangements of the light.
See the innocents, my sisters,
the clumsy ones, the laughing ones,
the rolled-up sleeves and the flapping shorts,
there is even a kilt (god of the midges,
you are good to us!) So gather your forces,
leave your tree trunks, forsake the rushes,
fly up from the sour brown mosses
to the sweet flesh of face and forearm.
Think of your eggs. What does the egg need?
Blood, and blood. Blood is what the egg needs.
Our men have done their bit, they've gone,
it was all they were good for, poor dears. Now

it is up to us. The egg is quietly screaming
for supper, blood, supper, blood, supper!
Attack, my little Draculas, my Amazons!
Look at those flailing arms and stamping feet.
They're running, swatting, swearing, oh they're hopeless.
Keep at them, ladies. This is a feast.
This is a midsummer night's dream.
Soon we shall all lie down filled and rich,
and lay, and lay, and lay, and lay, and lay.

Edwin Morgan

Magpie

One is sorrow, two is mirth,
three a wedding, four a birth,
five heaven, six hell,
seven's the de'il's ain sel!

Traditional

Crocodile

When doukin in the River Nile
I met a muckle crocodile.
He flicked his tail, he blinked his ee,
Syne bared his ugsome teeth at me.

Says I, 'I never saw the like.
Cleanin your teeth maun be a fyke!
What sort of besom do ye hae
To brush a set o teeth like thae?'

The crocodile said, 'Nane ava.
I never brush my teeth at aa!
A wee bird redds them up, ye see,
And saves me monie a dentist's fee.'

J. K. Annand

An Daolag Shìonach

Ann an ceàrn àraidh de Shìona,
san iar-dheas, chan fhada bho bheanntan Iunnàn,
tha seòrsa ùbhlan rim faighinn
a tha cho anabarrach taitneach
's gum biodh na h-ìompairean o shean a' cosg
an òir rin ceannach, is gan tairgse
aig fèisdean 's cuirmeannan san àros mhòr.
Ach cha robh dìreach blas nan ubhal aca.
Leugh mi gu robh daolag coireach ri sin,
nach fhaighear ach air craobhan na ceàirn ud,
's a dh'fhàgas uighean airson tràth a' chinntinn
an cridhe nan ubhal. Chan fhan iad ann
gu fad', ach thèid cùbhraidheachd iongantach
a sgaoileadh feadh gach meas. An dèidh don chnuimh
a sgiathan a shìneadh a-mach is teicheadh,
chan fhàgar lorg de fhantainn ann ach sgleò
òmarach an lì an ubhail, 's boladh
mìorbhaileach a dh'fhairtlich e
air sgoilearan is gàirnealairean
na cùirt gu lèir a mhìneachadh.

'S e sin a nì mi leis a' chànain seo.

Christopher Whyte

The Chinese Beetle

In a certain region of China,
in the south-west, not far from the mountains of Yunnan,
a kind of apple is to be found
with such an exquisite flavour
that in ancient times the emperors would spend
their gold to buy them, and offer them
at feasts and banquets in the great palace.
But they didn't actually taste like apples.
I read that this was because of a beetle
which is only found on the trees of that region
and which lays its eggs for the time of their growing
in the hearts of the apples. They do not stay
for long, but a marvellous fragrance
spreads through each fruit. After the worm
has spread its wings and fled
no trace remains of its sojourn
except an amber glow in the flesh
of the apple and a wonderful aroma
that all the scholars and gardeners
of the court were unable to explain.

That is what I do with this language.

Christopher Whyte

Do-it-Yourself Nature Poem

Autumn

De-dum-de-dum-de leaves of brown
De-dum-de-dum-de fluttering down
De-dum-de-dum-de-dum-de conkers
De-dum-de-dum-de-dum-de bonkers

Winter

De-dum-de-dum-de in the snow
De-dum-de-dum-de sledges go
De-dum-de-dum-de ice and sleet
De-dum-de-dum-de freezing feet

Spring

De-dum-de-dum-de crocus flowers
De-dum-de-dum-de April showers
De-dum-de-dum-de squelchy smelly
De-dum-de-dum-de slug in welly

Summer

De-dum-de-dum-de cricket bats
De-dum-de-dum-de floppy hats
De-dum-de-dum-de honey teas
De-dum-de-dum-de killer bees

John Whitworth

Scottish Haiku

A bonny Ayrshire
chews the cud on Ben Nevis –
noo *that's* a high coo!

John Rice

The Magic of an Otherworld

'God be between me and every fairy,
Every ill wish and every druidry.'

Fairy rune

Wee Davie Daylicht

Wee Davie Daylicht keeks[1] owre the sea,
Early in the mornin', wi' a clear e'e;
Waukens[2] a' the birdies that are sleepin' soun'.
Wee Davie Daylicht is nae lazy loon.

Wee Davie Daylicht glow'rs owre the hill,
Glints through the greenwood, dances on the rill;
Smiles on the wee cot, shines on the ha'[3];
Wee Davie Daylicht cheers the hearts o' a'.

Come bonnie bairnie, come awa' to me;
Cuddle in my bosie[4], sleep upon my knee.
Wee Davie Daylicht noo has closed his e'e.
In amang the rosy clouds, far ayont the sea.

Robert Tennant

1 peeks   2 wakens   3 small house, hall   4 bosum

Auld Daddy Darkness

Auld Daddy Darkness creeps frae his hole,
Black as a blackamoor, blin' as a mole;
Stir the fire till it lowes, let the bairnie sit,
Auld Daddy Darkness is no' wantit yet.

See him in the corners hidin' frae the licht,
See him at the window gloomin' at the nicht;
Turn up the gas licht, close the shutters a',
An' Auld Daddy Darkness will flee far awa'.

Awa' to hide the birdie within its cosy nest,
Awa' to hap the wee flooers on their mither's breast,
Awa' to loosen Gaffer Toil frae his daily ca',
For Auld Daddy Darkness is kindly to a'.

He comes when we're weary to wean's frae oor waes,
He comes when the bairnies are gettin' aff their claes,
To cover them sae cosy, an' bring bonnie dreams,
So Auld Daddy Darkness is better than he seems.

Shut yer een, my wee tot, you'll see Daddy then;
He's in below the bed claes, to cuddle ye he's fain.
Noo nestle in his bosie, sleep an' dream yer fill,
Till Wee Davy Daylicht comes keekin' owre the hill.

James Ferguson

Willie Winkie

Wee Willie Winkie rins through the town,
Up stairs and doon stairs in his nicht-gown,
Tirling[1] at the window, crying at the lock,
'Are the weans in their bed, for it's now ten o'clock?'

'Hey, Willie Winkie, are ye coming ben?
The cat's singing grey thrums to the sleeping hen,
The dog's spelder'd[2] on the floor, and disna gie a cheep,
But here's a waukrife[3] laddie, that winna fa' asleep.'

Onything but sleep, you rogue! glow'ring like the moon,
Rattling in an airn[4] jug wi' an airn spoon,
Rumbling, tumbling round about, crawing like a cock,
Skirling[5] like a kenna-what, wauk'ning sleeping fock.

'Hey, Willie Winkie – the wean's in a creel[6],
Wambling[7] aff a bodie's knee like a very eel,
Rugging[8] at the cat's lug, and ravelling a' her thrums –
Hey, Willie Winkie – see, there he comes!'

Wearied is the mither that has a stoorie⁹ wean,
A wee stumpie stoussie¹⁰, that canna rin his lane¹¹,
That has a battle aye wi' sleep before he'll close an e'e –
But a kiss frae aff his rosy lips gies strength anew to me.

William Miller

*1 tapping   2 stretched out   3 wakeful   4 iron   5 screaming   6 in a tizzie
7 writhing off   8 tugging   9 hyperactive   10 plump child   11 run by himself*

The Lady with the Book

2 fellows years back
now, one marching season
they joined up full whack
for their own reasons

one of them, a white-haired man
age about fifty-one
with him came a younger man
that was his sister's son

all through the winter that year
nights long and chill
they were sent out with good guns
marked men to kill

there's many done the same
where they lived was here and there
and where their orders came

as you travel about the world, people tell you things
and as this story goes, the young fellow began to
dream
every night the same dream

a beautiful lady dressed all in white
would walk towards him, a black book in her arm
kind of like a Bible
she'd open it to the first page, hold it out to him to
read
and there the names of those they'd killed were written
in neat rows
but she'd never turn the page
this is what he'd ask her: turn the page
she never would
till one night she did
and at the top of that page read clear
his uncle's name

the next night they were ordered out
a night of hard frost
there was a truck come hurtling down a bend
all the world stopped

the young man woke in hospital
in a clean and narrow bed
they said he'd never walk again
his uncle he was dead

if you'd have been where I have been
you might have seen him there
a quiet man in a city park
in his wheelchair

what of the lady all in white?
he said of her I dream no more
take the story, make a song
they'll think you're lying for sure.

Robin Williamson

Performing Doll

No fairground ballerina she
With eyes like saucers
Inward spinning.
A demented doll
Taller than a tree.
Hooped round her concertina pleats
And corrugated frill
A rim of children cling.
They hold hands and their breath
And wait.   The thrill begins.
From somewhere hidden in her heart
Sparks fly, the levers shunt.
And round and round she rolls
Flips up her skirt à la can-can
On each gyration.   Screams
Of bright fear whirl
And spill into the night
Like catherine wheels.
The grown-ups on the ground
Have seen and heard it all before
And before long their gaze strays
    To the automatic kick
    Of monstrous lead-lined knickers.

Dilys Rose

Wee Jenny

Opposite our granny's in Mansion Street, Possilpark,
Wee Jenny appears at her top floor window
on a Sunday best chapeled morning.

There she is, a tiny woman in her green dress,
a brooch above her heart, and might that be
a spinning wheel behind her?
She has no shadow.

Wee Jenny's on the rockinghorse,
Wee Jenny's in the mill.
Wee Jenny's in the caravan,
Wee Jenny's in the hill.

For they say Wee Jenny spends all day
stitching and sewing, sewing and stitching.
Never raises her head, never blinks a star eye,
mends and makes, makes and mends.
Thimbles clashing and all the whiles
hiding her humfy-back.

Until Sunday when she sits at the open window,
waves to neighbours, across to our gran, to the children.
Throws doon a jam piece in a white bag,
or might have done if the children hadn't teased so.

At teatime,
goes back inside to dream of silver threads
piercing golden buttons that are sprinkled and sparkle
on her little girl coat to capture the glint
of fairy eyes in dashing flight above
the foundries and engineering works
of Glasgow's northern outskirts.

And did she sail across the canal in an eggshell?
And was that eggshell pierced?

> *Wee Jenny's on the rockinghorse,*
> *Wee Jenny's in the mill.*
> *Wee Jenny's in the Clyde canal,*
> *Wee Jenny's in the hill.*

John Rice

Escape at Bedtime

The lights from the parlour and kitchen shone out
   Through the blinds and the windows and bars;
And high overhead and all moving about,
   There were thousands of millions of stars.

There ne'er were such thousands of leaves on a tree,
   Nor of people in church or the Park,
As the crowds of the stars that looked down upon me,
   And that glittered and winked in the dark.

The Dog, and the Plough, and the Hunter, and all,
   And the star of the sailor, and Mars,
These shone in the sky, and the pail by the wall,
   Would be half full of water and stars.

They saw me at last, and they chased me with cries,
   And they soon had me packed into bed;
But the glory kept shining and bright in my eyes,
   And the stars going round in my head.

Robert Louis Stevenson

Dreamscape at Bedtime

(after RLS)

The lichts frae the harbour and ferries shone oot
    frae the cafes, amusements and bars;
whilst high owreheid a' movin' aboot
    there were thoosans an' millions o' stars.

The beams frae the lichthoose sprayed owre the sea,
    a ship had white een lik' a shark.
An' the pattern o' planets poored their pure licht on me
    as they glimmered and winked in the dark.

The Great Bear and Venus, the Plough and the moon
    were torches that lit up the nicht;
and the waater was speckled lik' an auld table spoon
    reflectin' a cauld, siller licht.

I woke up at last fu' o' wonder and sighs
    to find I wis waarm in ma bed;
but the marvel kept spinnin' and clear in ma een,
    an' the stars going roon' in ma head.

John Rice

Three Riddles

1.

The man who made it
Did not want it.
The man who bought it did not need it.
The man who used it never saw it.
What was it?

Answer: a coffin.

2.

In marble hall as white as milk
My lining is as soft as silk.
No doors or windows in my stronghold,
Yet thieves break in and steal my gold.
What am I?

Answer: a white hen's egg.

3.

You go in through one door,
You come out through three,
And when you're in, you're ready for out,
And when you're out, you're ready for in!
What am I?

Answer: a jumper.

Duncan Williamson

The Great Silkie of Sule Skerry

An earthly nourris sits and sings,
    And aye she sings, 'Ba, lily wean!
Little ken I my bairnis father,
    Far less the land that he staps in.'

Then ane arose at her bed-fit,
    An' a grumly guest I'm sure was he:
'Here am I, thy bairnis father,
    Although that I be not comelie.

'I am a man, upo the lan,
    An' I am a silkie in the sea;
And when I'm far and far frae lan,
    My dwelling is in Sule Skerrie.'

'It was na weel,' quo the maiden fair,
    'It was na weel, indeed,' quo she,
'That the Great Silkie of Sule Skerrie
    Suld hae come and aught a bairn to me.'

Now he has taen a purse of goud,
　　And he has pat it upo her knee,
Sayin', 'Gie to me my little young son,
　　An' tak thee up thy nourris-fee.

'An' it sall come to pass on a simmer's day,
　　When the sin shines het on evera stane,
That I will tak my little young son,
　　An' teach him for to swim the faem.

'An' thu sall marry a proud gunner,
　　An' a proud gunner I'm sure he'll be,
An' the very first schot that ere he schoots,
　　He'll schoot baith my young son and me.'

Traditional

Songs and Sadness

'Bright is the ring of words
When the right man rings them,
Fair the fall of songs
When the singer sings them.'

Robert Louis Stevenson

There Was a Sang

There was a sang
That aye I wad be singin',
There was a star,
An' clear it used tae shine;
An' liltin' in the starlicht
Thro' the shadows
I gaed lang syne.

There was a sang;
But noo, I canna mind it.
    There was a star,
But noo, it disna shine.
There was a luve that led me
Thro' the shadows –
And it *was* mine.

Helen B. Cruickshank

Isle of Islay

How high
the gulls fly
o'er Islay.
How sad
the farm lad
deep in play.

Felt like a seed on your land.

How well
the sheep's bell
music makes.
Roving the cliff
when fancy
takes.

Felt like a grain on your sand.

How blessed
the forest
with bird song.
How neat
the cut peat
laid so long.

Felt like a seed on your land.

How high
the gulls fly
o'er Islay.
How sad
the farm lad
deep in play.

Felt like grain on your sand,
felt like a seed on your land,
felt like a tide left me here.

Donovan Leitch

Dance to Your Daddy,
My Bonnie Laddie

Dance to your daddy, my bonnie laddie,
Dance to your daddy till the boat comes in;
And you'll get a fishie in a wee dishie
If you dance to your daddy till the boat comes in.

(attributed to) William Watson, Newcastle

Grib to Your Naiskel,
My Beenship Kinchen

Grib to your naiskel, my beenship kinchen,
Grib to your naiskel till the beerie bings anee;
You'll feek a flattrin in a wee mahzie
If you'll grib to your naiskel till the beerie bings anee.

*Cathie Higgins' version in the cant,
the private language of the Travellers.*

O That I Had Ne'er Been Married

O that I had ne'er been married,
   I wad never had nae care.
Now I've gotten wife and bairns
   They cry 'crowdie'[1] evermair.

Ance crowdie, twice crowdie,
   Three times crowdie in a day:
Gin ye crowdie ony mair
   Ye'll crowdie a' my meal away!

Traditional

[1] *thick oatmeal gruel*

Dazzledance

I have an eye of silver,
I have an eye of gold,
I have a tongue of reed-grass
and a story to be told.

I have a hand of metal,
I have a hand of clay,
I have two arms of granite
and a song for every day.

I have a foot of damson,
I have a foot of corn,
I have two legs of leaf-stalk
and a dance for every morn.

I have a dream of water,
I have a dream of snow,
I have a thought of wildfire
and a harp-string long and low.

I have an eye of silver,
I have an eye of gold,
I have a tongue of reed-grass
and a story to be told.

John Rice

Paddy on the Railway

Paddy on the railway pickin' up stones,
By came an engine and broke Paddy's bones;
'Ach,' says Paddy, 'that's no' fair.'
'Well,' says the engine-man, 'ye shouldnae be there!'

Traditional

Hometime

When my grandfather died he saw,
he said, not Death's bare head, but aunts,
his antique aunts in crackling black,
come to call him back from play.

Kate Clanchy

A St Kilda Lament

It was no crew of landsmen
Crossed the ferry on Wednesday;
'Tis tidings of disaster if you live not.

What has kept you so long from me?
Are the high sea and the sudden wind catching you,
So that you could not at once give her sail?

'Tis a profitless journey
That took the noble men away,
To take our one son from me and from Donald.

My son and my three brothers are gone,
And the one son of my mother's sister,
And, sorest tale, that will come or has come, my hus-
band.

What has set me to draw ashes
And to take a spell at digging
Is that the men are away with no word of their living.

I am left without fun or merriment
Sitting on the floor of the glen;
My eyes are wet, oft are tears on them.

Anon.

Note:

In 1865 Alexander Carmichael collected some songs from the the St Kilda poet Euphemia MacCrimmon. She was 84 years old at the time. More than likely the people of St Kilda could draw on a wonderful heritage of stories, poems and songs. However, very few poems and songs from St Kilda now exist as the reciting of poems, the telling of stories, dancing and music making were banned by the missionaries who went there. This surviving song lyric was written by an island woman. In it she laments the loss of all the menfolk in her family who have been lost at sea in a boating tragedy.

People, Places

'My grannie says her grannie
Kent monie a tale and rhyme
That noo my grannie tells
To me at my bedtime.'

from 'Auld Farrant'
by J. K. Annand (1908–1993)

Ye Cannae Shove Yer Granny Aff a Bus

Oh ye cannae shove yer granny aff a bus,
ye cannae shove yer granny aff a bus.
　　Oh ye cannae shove yer granny
　　fur she's yer mammy's mammy,
oh, ye cannae shove yer granny aff a bus.

Ye can shove yer other granny aff a bus,
ye can shove yer other granny aff a bus.
　　Oh ye can shove yer other granny
　　fur she's jist yer daddy's mammy,
oh, ye can shove yer other granny aff a bus.

Traditional

Bedtime Story

'I don't like that one, Hansel
and Gretel, I told them so, little
children enticed by a wicked witch
into her marzipan cottage – such
goings-on – too fearsome
for words, just before bedtime
too: keep them up half the night.'

They recognise her plight,
interpret it differently:
Grandma would be upset, you see
they confide later, from tact:
it's the old woman who gets cooked.

Stewart Conn

Voodoo for Miss Maverick

I dinna like Miss Maverick –
This cushion's for her heid.
I'm jumpin' aa my wecht on't,
An noo Miss Maverick's deid!

Ye're deid, ye're deid, Miss Maverick,
An never mair ye'll say
I dance like a hird o' Ayrshire
Ky on a mercat day!

I'll pit ye ablaw the sofa –
Ye're deid an yirdit baith,
An never mair ye'll miscaa me –
Ye've drawn yer hinmaist braith!

Sandy Thomas Ross

Knee-high to a Poem

The way a four-year-old enters the room
By stealth to pick up a pair of, say,
Toy binoculars and looks at the wall
But really is listening to the adults

Saying nothing at all
Worth staying around for and goes:
That's how the heartbeat of a poem
Keeps us on our toes.

James McGonigal

Best Pal

I have stayed the night at Charmaine's
loads of times,
but she has never ever stayed at mine's.

I have asked her mother week upon week
no luck –
'maybe another day,' is all she'll say.

Last night Charmaine finally came.
In her bag,
a rubber sheet we spread on my bed.

Now I know Charmaine wets the bed,
we are close,
closer than before, close as sisters.

Jackie Kay

Sarah: Fed Up

See ma mammy,
says eat yer dinner.
Gies me cabbidge.
See ma granny,
says the wean
wullnae eat that,
leave it, hen.
Gies me choclit.
See ma daddy,
says ah've goatie
clear ma plate.
Dinnae like that
greasy gravy,
stane cauld tatties.
See ma granda,
says the bairn
s'no goat a stummick
like a coo.
Gies me lickris,
pandrops, chews.
Ett thum aw.

Feel seek noo.

Janet Paisley

Rewriting Childhood

I am rewriting my childhood,
holding it up to my eye
like a jam jar of sticklebacks.

Sunlight catches the glass –
the fish flash crimson and silver
as they twist and gasp
in a dazzle of golden light.

I carried it home,
the secret of life in a jam jar.

I am rewriting my childhood,
editing out the next day
and the day after
when the grey-brown sticklebacks
hung belly-upwards
in a cloud of watered-down milk.

James Aitchison

A Boy's Song

Where the pools are bright and deep
Where the grey trout lies asleep
Up the river and o'er the lea
That's the way for Billy and me

Where the blackbird sings the latest
Where the hawthorn blooms the sweetest
Where the nestlings plentiest be
That's the way for Billy and me

Where the mowers mow the cleanest
Where the hay lies thick and greenest
There to trace the homeward bee
That's the way for Billy and me

Where the poplar grows the smallest
Where the old pine waves the tallest
'Pies and rooks know who are we
That's the way for Billy and me

Where the hazel bank is steepest
Where the shadow falls the deepest
There the clustering nuts fall free
That's the way for Billy and me

Why the boys should drive away
Little sweet maidens from the play
Or love to tear and fight so well
That's the thing I never could tell

But this I know I love to play
Through the meadow among the hay
Up the water and o'er the lea
That's the way for Billy and me.

James Hogg
'The Ettrick Shepherd'

The Bonnie Broukit Bairn

(for Peggy)

Mars is braw in crammasy[1],
Venus in a green silk goun,
The auld mune shak's her gowden feathers,
Their starry talk's a wheen o' blethers[2],

Nane for thee a thochtie sparin',
Earth, thou bonnie broukit bairn[3]!
– *But greet[4], an' in your tears ye'll drown*
The haill clanjamfrie[5]!

Hugh MacDiarmid
(Christopher Murray Grieve)

---

1 fine in crimson   2 a lot of nonsense   3 neglected child   4 weep
5 the whole of worthless humanity

Wee Jamie

Wee Jamie, a canny young Scot,
Observed, when the kettle was hot,
   That the steam raised the lid,
And it's thanks to this kid
   That you and I know Watt's watt.

Joyce Johnson

The Blue Jacket

When there comes a flower to the stingless nettle,
    To the hazel bushes, bees,
I think I can see my little sister
    Rocking herself by the hazel trees.

Rocking her arms for very pleasure
    That every leaf so sweet can smell,
And that she has on her the warm blue jacket
    Of mine, she liked so well.

Oh to win near you, little sister!
    To hear your soft lips say –
'I'll never tak' up wi' lads or lovers,
    But a baby I maun hae.

'A baby in a cradle rocking,
    Like a nut, in a hazel shell,
And a new blue jacket, like this o' Annie's,
    It sets me aye sae well.'

Marion Angus

So Shy

He was so shy he was born with a caul,
sort of a shawl made from the membrane
of the womb. He was tongue-tied;

so shy he kept a dummy in his mouth
for two years; then, when that went,
a thumb. He was wide-eyed, dumb; so shy

he would hide in the cupboard under the stairs
for hours, with a bear; hearing his name called
from the top to the bottom of the house, quiet

as a mouse; shy as the milk in a coconut,
shy as a slither of soap. When he got dressed,
he wore shy clothes – a balaclava, mitts.

He ate shy food – blancmange, long-lasting mints.
He drank shy drinks – juice from a cup
with a lid and a lip, sip by shy sip.

He was so shy he lived with a blush,
sort of a flush under the skin, like the light
behind curtains on windows when somebody's in.

Carol Ann Duffy

Seize the Day

Come on, Daddy, come now, I hear them shout
as I put the finishing touches to this and that

in the safe confines of my study:
Hurry, Daddy, before it's too late, we're ready!

They are so right. Now is the time.
It won't wait, on that you can bet your bottom

dollar. So rouse yourself, get the drift
before you're muffled and left

for useless. *Let's build a snowman, then
a snow-woman to keep him company. When*

*that's finished, and with what's left over,
a giant snowball that will last for ever,*

only hurry, Daddy. As soon as this poem
is finished, I promise, I'll come –

essential first, to pin down what is felt.
Meanwhile, the snow begins to melt.

Stewart Conn

a quiet daughter

they found me in the corner
way at the back
of my mother's wardrobe

at first they thought i was a button
broken loose from a frayed thread
or a mothball, happy in the dark

then, as i grew, they thought i was
a shoe without a partner, but
they were busy folk – it was easier
to poke me back beside the fallen
jumpers and the missing socks

as for me, i was quite content
tucked up in the folds of mother's frocks

from time to time she'd drag me out
wear me, dangled prettily
on the end of her arm –
the ultimate accessory
a quiet daughter

Magi Gibson

Easter Eggs

My sister
brought her budgies home
for Easter

one green, one blue,
beaks sharper than
they looked,

quick little things.
I only pulled the door
a single inch –

a single inch
was all it took. No budgies left.
The door blew open

(yes, the wide back door).
Those budgies flew right up into the sky,
into the sharp, cool blue. I

called. They didn't listen;
left behind blue feathers, and green down
and husks of millet.

I knew my sister wouldn't like it.
That's why I've left these chocolate eggs
propped up in the cage . . .

Anne MacLeod

Sharleen: Ah'm Shy

Ah'm shy. Aye, ah am.
Cannae look naebody in the eye.
Ah've seen me go in a shoap
an jist hope naebody wid talk tae me.
Things that happen, likesae,
ye're oot fur a walk an some bloke
whit's nivir even spoke afore goes by
an he's givin ye the eye.
See me, ah jist waant tae die.
Ah go rid tae the roots ae ma hair.
Weel, it's no fair, is it?
Feel a right twit.
See ma Ma. She says it'll pass.
'Ye'll grow oot ae it, hen.'
Aye, aw richt, bit when?
Ye kin git awfy fed up
bein the local beetroot.
So, last time ah went oot
– tae the disco –
ah bocht this white make-up.
White lightnin, it sayd.
Ah thocht 'nae the beamers the night.
This stuff'll see me aw right.'
Onywey, there ah wis, actin it.
Daen ma pale an interestin bit.

White lightnin?
See unner them flashin lights –
it wis quite frightnin.
Cause ma face looked aw blue.
Och, see whin ah think ae it noo,
it wis mortifyin
cause they aw thocht ah wis dyin
an they dialled 999.
Fine thing tae be,
centre ae awbody's attention. Me.
They hud me in sut oan this chair
bit whin they brocht strechers in
ah slid oantae the flair
an jist lay there.
Ah thocht, rule number wan,
whin ye've made a fool ae yersell
dinnae lit oan, play the gemme.
So ah let oot a groan an lay still,
until this ambulance fella feels ma wrist
an then he gies ma neck a twist an
– ye'll no believe this –
bit right there an then,
he gies me a kiss.
Blew intae ma mooth, honest!
God'strewth, ah wis gaspin fur braith.
  Jist goes tae show ye're no safe,

naeplace, these days.
Onywey, ah blew right back.
That made him move quick.
An he says 'Ur you aw richt?
Ur ye gaun tae be sick?'
That's whin ah noticed his eyes.
They wur daurk broon
an starin right intae thum
made ma stomach go roon.
Ah felt kinda queer an he says
'C'mon hen, we'll get ye ootae here.'
Bit ah made him take me right hame.
Though ah'm seein him again.
The morra. Aw the same,
how kin ah tell him, dae ye suppose,
that whin ye kiss a lassie,
ye dinnae haud hur nose?

Janet Paisley

Moral Philosophy

whiji *mean* whiji mean

lissn
noo lissnty mi toknty yi
right

h hawd oan
whair wuzza
naw

aye
whitsiz name
him way thi
yi no yon

here
here yoo
yir no eevn lissnin
name a god

a doant no

Tom Leonard

The Story of Our Street

The girl's left hand keeps her coat shut, the other's
empty. She's standing in the middle of the street,
the traffic braking to a stop around her.
Hardly sixteen: bleached hair, bleached skin, fear.

The man she's with: badly healing cuts and anger
clenched into a face, pressed-in bruises
where the eyes should be.
She's telling him she's sorry, and being sworn at.

Nearby, a parliament of two men and a woman sits
    arguing
upon the pavement; they shout at her to grow up,
can't she? A taxi horn blares –
she doesn't move. It's raining.

I drop my 50p into the parliamentary cup, and walk
    past.
Behind me, the street shuts like a book, the place
    marked
just at the point where he hits her
in the mouth.

When I'm back this evening the story will have moved
    on:
there will be no girl, no man and no parliament
                            – only you and I
and everyone else, and the street around us growing
    darker
as the sun abandons it.

Ron Butlin

Purity

seen on the Meadows, Edinburgh

When I make a picture
I will put a black man
in bold headlines
running full-scale across the Meadows –

beside him a white dog
husky and blurred
in wavy outlines
skating the grassy surface in circles.

Sharp-edged, bright-black
tropical man . . .
snow-soft, stark-white
arctic dog . . .
superimposed on the antique Meadows.

Trees are tense to the roots,
grass stretches, stones stare
from medical buildings,
as these two in their extreme purity
cut across our Middle Meadow Walk.

Tessa Ransford

Belly-button

Lying in the bath,
I look at it, this genealogical twirl.

It connects me,
matrilineally of course,
to Morag daughter of Morag daughter of Peggy
    daughter of Catriona Mhòr,
who once sailed, single-handed,
in a home-made canoe
between Eigg and Barra.

She was bringing home a sack of meal.

Through that severed fleshy tube
I drank my mother's poverty,
as she, in turn, had swallowed
her own mother's poverty,
and so on and so on.

The rich strawberry foam covers my starved history.

Angus Peter Campbell

The Image o' God

Crawlin' aboot like a snail in the mud,
    Covered wi' clammy blae[1],
ME, made after the image o' God –
    Jings! but it's laughable, tae.

Howkin'[2] awa' 'neath a mountain o' stane,
    Gaspin' for want o' air,
The sweat makin' streams doon my bare back-bane
    And my knees a' hauckit and sair[3].

Strainin' and cursin' the hale shift through,
    Half-starved, half-blin', half-mad;
And the gaffer he says, 'Less dirt in that coal
    Or ye go up the pit, my lad!'

So I gi'e my life to the Nimmo squad
    For eicht and fower a day;
Me! made after the image o' God –
    Jings! but it's laughable, tae.

Joe Corrie

1 blue mud   2 digging   3 hacked and sore

Scatter-brained Chances

We grow and vanish
          down dark lovers' lanes
Where the shackles of innocence
          go up in flames.

Here passion's forthcoming
          as desire runs strong
And everyone's caught
          in the eye of life's storm.

With a pressing of flesh
          we devour and discover
In the name of true love –
          that immaculate cover.

It's simply amazing,
          all cradle days gone –
We transform forever
          into adults by dawn.

When all passion has climaxed
          and the dastardly's done –
Enter blind panic
          along with the sun.

For all shrouded in darkness
                     a third party sits –
Unused in a packet
                     purchased cheap at the Ritz.

Charlotte Munro

The Royal High School

After the children had gone
the gulls came, in a white flit:
sentinel at windows,
falling between buildings.
The janitors and cleaners never saw them
dropping in: ambling down corridors,
looking into rooms, blinking
at their new estate.
They nest here now, among the jotters
and pencils, unopened boxes
of *The Scottish Constitution*;
living like kings
on a diet of silverfish,
long-life milk and chalk.

Robin Robertson

Note:

Had the 1979 referendum succeeded in bringing Scottish devolution, the proposed seat of parliament was the old Royal High School on Calton Hill, which had been standing empty for years, and is empty still – overlooking the new, purpose-built parliament at Holyrood.

Yesterday, Today and Tomorrow

'The year unhinges
and all possibility is there
holding its white morning breath
outside an opening door.'

Janet Paisley

A Celtic History

I'm tellt the auncient Celts collectit heids
like some fowks gaither stamps,
an gin ye were their guest wad shaw ye kists
fou o their latest prizes.
Nou we're delivirt frae sic ugsome weys
we scrieve lists o the scunnersomely deid
prentit in black and white.
Yon's faur mair hygenic and forbye
ye can get a lot mair in than ye can in a kist.

I'm tellt the auncient Celts focht in bare scud . . .
Man . . . *yon*'s a mark o unco determination.
Ye've shairly got tae ken whit ye're fechtin *fur*
tae tak the haill Roman Empire on in yir buff.
Gin they'd taen Hitler, Napoleon and aa the lave
o the born leaders o sufferan mankind
and gart thaim fecht in nocht but their drawers and
    semmits
yon wad hae been a solid move towards peace.

William Neill

165

Dumpling

Make way for the dumpling, the hero
of a Scottish kitchen's history at last.
Let us celebrate the hero dumpling,
rolled through two world wars to feed us.
Mummified in muslins, hung in clooties,
boiled for years in brilloed jeely-pans
and swathed in a fat ghost of steam.
Sedater of the nation, the dumpling
has weighed upon the bellies of kings
and beggars alike – and will again.
Rich with the sweet, ancient raisins
of our great-great grannies' eyes.
Studded with our great-great grandads'
hard brass threepenny-bit teeth.
Here he comes, here comes the hero:
this colossal arse of a pudding
like a monster's benappied bairn.
Solid as a medicine ball, but riddled
with everyday riches: the fat
of an ox's kidneys, this poulticed
bomb of spice and suet and sweat
will keep for weeks, months, years –
it will last a lifetime of thrift,
wrapped in greaseproof, lardered,

taken out to be sliced and fried.
Here is the hero dumpling at last:
so slap the hero, slap him hard
give the hero's arse a good, hard slap.

Brian McCabe

Gollop's

Gollop was our grandmother's butcher.
Saying his name out loud, you swallowed
a lump of gristle whole. Even the thought
of going to Gollop's made us gulp,
made my little green-eyed sister's eyes
grow rounder, greener. Swags of rabbits
dangled at the door in furry curtains;
their eyes milky, blood congealed
around their mouths like blackcurrant jelly.
You'd to run a gauntlet of paws.

Inside, that smell of blood and sawdust
still in my nostrils. Noises. The thump
as a cleaver fell; flinchings, aftershocks
as sinews parted, bone splintered.
The wet rasp of a saw. My eyes
were level with the chopping bench.
Its yellow wood dipped in the middle
like the bed I shared with Rosy.
Sometimes a trapdoor in the floor
was folded back. Through clouds of frost
our eyes made out wooden steps, then
huge shapes shawled in ice – the cold-store.

Into which the butcher fell,
once, bloody apron and all.
When my grandparents went to see
Don Juan, and told us how it ended
– *Like Mr Gollop!* I whispered.
Mr Gollop only broke his leg, but
   Crash! Bang! Wallop!
   Went Mr Gollop!
we chanted from our sagging bed,
giggles celebrating his downfall,
cancelling his nasty shop.
As the Co-op did a few years later
when it opened on the High Street.
Giving him the chop.

Anna Crowe

Border Raids

(for my grandmother)

Fierce pins plough her hair
You can tell by the angry drag
of the net
that once she was beautiful,
envied and glad of it
The nightingale of the county,
electrifying the village halls

She told me she wore winged hats
tall as gladioli,
and the hanging moon sang with her,
and how they clapped and horded
at her doors

When she went,
she went like the old bunch, cursing,
blue as smoke,
you could almost smell the burning
(Oh, they were a wild lot, the Johnstones,
border raiders,
horse stealers setting the Kirk alight
and all their enemies inside)

With her heart tattered
as a tyre on the road
she begged for morphine
and to be done with it,
to be gone among the gliding dead

She glints now in the gooseberry bushes,
her broom hisses out at low-dashing cats
In the night she slaps up her window
and hurls hairbrushes

I've been thinking
If I could go back,
stealing up the cemetery hill
to borrow back her bones,
I'd give her to the merry gods
of the midsummer garden
who dance among the columbines
who fib and fart
and I'd tell them to trumpet her out

Alison Fell

View of Scotland/Love Poem

Down on her hands and knees
at ten at night on Hogmanay,
my mother still giving it elbowgrease
jiffywaving the vinolay. (This is too
ordinary to be nostalgia.) On the kitchen table
a newly opened tin of sockeye salmon.
Though we do not expect anyone,
the slab of black bun,
petticoat-tails fanned out
on bone china.
'Last year it was very quiet . . .'

Mum's got her rollers in with waveset
and her well-pressed good dress
slack across the candlewick upstairs.
Nearly half-ten already and her not shifted!
If we're to even hope to prosper
this midnight must find us
how we would like to be.
A new view of Scotland
with a dangling calendar
is propped under last year's,
ready to take its place.

Darling, it's thirty years since
anybody was able to trick me,
December thirtyfirst, into
'looking into a mirror to see a lassie
wi' as minny heids as days in the year' –
and two already since,
familiar strangers at a party,
we did not know that we were
the happiness we wished each other
when the Bells went, did we?

All over the city
off-licences pull down their shutters.
People make for where they want to be
to bring the New Year in.
In highrises and tenements
sunburst clocks tick
on dusted mantelshelves.
Everyone puts on their best spread of plenty
(for to even hope to prosper
this midnight must find us
how we would like to be).
So there's a bottle of sickly liqueur
among the booze in the alcove,
golden crusts on steak pies
like quilts on a double bed.

And this is where we live.
There is no time like the
present for a kiss.

Liz Lochhead

Coco Bendy

Coco Bendy had a wife,
    she was awfie dandy.
She fell in beneath the bed
    and tummled ower the chanty.

Coco Bendy he came in
    and smelt an awfie stink.
He went in beneath the bed
    and had a fizzy drink.

Traditional

Old Tongue

When I was eight, I was forced south.
Not long after, when I opened
my mouth, a strange thing happened.
I lost my Scottish accent.
Words fell off my tongue:
eedyit, dreich, wabbit, crabbit,
stummer, teuchter, heidbanger,
so you are, so am ur, see you, see ma ma,
shut yer geggie, or I'll gie you the malkie!

My own vowels started to stretch like my bones
and I turned my back on Scotland.
Words disappeared in the dead of night,
new words marched in: ghastly, awful,
quite dreadful, scones said like stones.
Pokey hats into ice-cream cones.
Oh where did all my words go –
my old words, my lost words?
Did you ever feel sad when you lost a word,
did you ever try and call it back
like calling in the sea?
If I could have found my words wandering,
I swear I would have taken them in,
swallowed them whole, knocked them back.

Out in the English soil, my old words
buried themselves. It made my mother's blood boil.
I cried one day with the wrong sound in my mouth.
I wanted them back; I wanted my old accent back,
my old tongue. My dour, soor Scottish tongue.
Sing-songy. *I wanted to gie it laldie.*

Jackie Kay

Guttersnipe

Richt ready wi her hands wis my mither,
nae doot because my faither
wis maistly hyne frae hame, and me a scamp.
Ae day, lat loose tae play,
I ventered ootby the cassied close
(bairnie-safe, near-at-hand)
tae fa in wi a brent-new freen
wi torn breeks and a clarty face.

He learnt me some braw new wirds
that dirlt and hottert in his mou
and mine. They soonded fine.
So baith thegither we tried them oot
and leuched and keckled doon the wynd.
Blythfu I shared them wi my mither,
expeckin a leuch or a hug,
but wis handed oot a weel-skelpt lug.

'Such expressions nice boys never utter.
They belong,' quo mither, 'in the gutter.'

Ken Morrice

When You See Millions of the Mouthless Dead

When you see millions of the mouthless dead
Across your dreams in pale battalions go,
Say not soft things as other men have said,
That you'll remember. For you need not so.
Give them not praise. For, deaf, how should they know
It is not curses heaped on each gashed head?
Nor tears. Their blind eyes see not your tears flow.
Nor honour. It is easy to be dead.
Say only this, 'They are dead.' Then add thereto,
'Yet many a better one has died before.'
Then, scanning all the o'ercrowded mass, should you
Perceive one face that you loved heretofore,
It is a spook. None wears the face you knew.
Great death has made all his for evermore.

Charles Hamilton Sorley

Note: In May 1915 Charles Hamilton Sorley crossed to France to serve in the trenches during the First World War. In October of that year he was killed in action at the Battle of Loos. He was twenty years old. He left only 37 complete poems. The one printed here is from Marlborough and Other Poems, a collection published three months after his death. The book became a popular and critical success during the 1920s and ran through six editions.

The Safeway Mountaineer

Stacking
shelves
with tins
of
sweet corn,
trying

to pull
overloaded pallets
you'll never move in
a thousand years
of mopping the floor with dirty lather
making it dirtier than before,
and getting a smile from pricegun girls,
checking all the cartons are straight
and not one jar is out
of place,
getting screamed at
by moustache-assistants
who stand for ages in front of
the mirror
getting the knots in their ties
JUST RIGHT,
watching

the sun
set outside
the window
long
distance
shepherd skies,
and getting a smile from checkout girls,
racing trolleys up car park ramps
jamming the lift to have
a drift
no one knowing where
you are,
climbing

a Silver Spoon sugar mountain,
waiting for someone to stroll along
and pull the crucial bag from
the bottom send you
tumbling

Graham Fulton

Port nan Carbad-Iarainn

Dithis
Charbad-iarainn
Ri taobh a chèile
'S iad an impis dèanamh às
Anns an dorchadas
Agus mi fhìn a' sealltainn
Air an taobh thall
'S mi an dùil
Gur h-e mo sgàth fhèin
A gheibh mi air ais
Anns a' ghlainne
'S clisgeadh orm 's uamhann
'S gun agam de sgàth
Ach coigreach air mo bheulaibh.

Rody Gorman

Two Trains

Two carriages side by side
About to depart in the darkness:

There's me
Looking into the other,

Expecting to find
My own reflection,

Shocked
To find not my own

But a stranger
Looking into my eyes.

Rody Gorman

Gazetteer

Stromeferry
(no ferry)

Stoneybridge
(no bridge)

Ullapool
(no pool)
at all)

Kirkintilloch
(no loch)

Portree
(no tree)

Gourock
(no rock)

Muir of Ord
(no ford)

Mitherwell
(no well)

Dingwall (no wall)
Redpoint (no point

Stornoway
(no way)

Aviemore
(no more)

Knockando
(do).

Rody Gorman

Saturday View

There are no ghosts in the air,
No voices in the wind
Combing the grass on the hill,
Scratching the old scalp of the earth,
But a lot is going on, in much the same way
As it ever has. The lights of the town,
Lights that float across the estuary,
Big lights of motorway interchanges
Glaring on the boundaries of the dark,
Are recent additions, that will pass,
Like service stations and shopping malls,
And Saturday crowds, free of the weather,
Closed off from the endless sky,
Browsing in packed aisles of plenty.

Mark Ogle

The Room

The room was plain and expensive,
stuck like a squint eye
in the College of Inquisitive Sheep.
The window witnessed well-behaved
sunsets, mischievous stars and
me.

And you.

There, on that dumb hard bed
I re-nightmared the hotpinintheeye
of laser surgery, I traced waterfalls
to source, I sent poems fireworking
enough to seduce you.

The room is exactly
as it was, the same sun sets,
the sheep might as well
be clones: only the mirror sincerely
remembers and does not know
what to make of me,
makes of me
something transparent, transient and old,
a blinding, trembling tear.

Kevin MacNeil

Burnt Car

Death to the melted glass
hanging into the windspace
like tongues of heated perspex.
But raspy as stones on a path.

What's left of the steering wheel
impales itself on its own column.
The seats are dark labyrinths
of black charred springs and things.

The top half of the windscreen
flops itself, as if it jumped,
like a Salvador Dali clock,
over the useless handbrake.

The radio lies dead beside the gearstick;
too cheap to be stolen.
The paint, heated to snowy whiteness
in the boot, is an avalanche.

The windscreen wipers droop,
like snakes' tongues,
onto the body, licking dust
in the worst of droughts.

A front tyre
intact in absurdity;
the wind, last night,
blew in its favour.

The wing mirror popped,
escaping the inferno,
as it roared the chromium
into purples and rainbows.

The number plate is missing,
presumed molten; the silver sick
below the anonymous grin
of the teethy radiator.

Des Dillon

Lucky Bag

Tattie scones, St Andra's banes,
a rod-and-crescent Pictish stane,
a field o whaups, organic neeps,
a poke o Brattisani's chips;
a clootie well, computer bits,
an elder o the wee free Kirk;

a golach fi Knoydart,
a shalwar-kemeez;
Dr Simpson's anaesthetics, zzzzzzzz,
a gloup, a clachan, a Broxburn bing,
a giro, a demo, Samye Ling;

a ro-ro in the gloaming,
a new-born Kirkaldy
baby-gro; a Free State, a midden,
a chambered cairn –
yer Scottish lucky-bag, one for each wean;
please form an orderly   rabble.

Kathleen Jamie

Last Lauch

The Minister said it wad dee
the cypress bush I plantit.
But the bush grew til a tree,
naething dauntit.

Hit's growin, stark and heich,
derk and straucht and sinister,
kirkyairdie-like and dreich.
But whaur's the Minister?

Douglas Young

Index of First Lines

Index of Poets

Acknowledgements

James Aitchison, 'Rewriting Childhood' from *Second Nature*, Aberdeen University Press, 1990. **Marion Angus,** 'The Blue Jacket' from *The Turn of the Day*, Porpoise Press/Faber & Faber, 1931. **J. K. Annand,** 'Crocodile' from *Bairn Rhymes, Scots Verse for Children*, Mercat Press, 1999. **Meg Bateman,** 'An deidh an Torraidh/The Day of the Funeral' from *Aotromachd agus dain eile/Lightness and Other Poems*, Polygon, 1997. **Robin Bell,** 'Luck', by permission of the author. **Sheena Blackhall,** 'Daddy-Lang-Legs', 'Snailie', by permission of the author. **George Mackay Brown,** 'Orkney: Whale Islands' and 'Island School' from *The Wreck of the Archangel*, John Murray (Publishers) Ltd, 1989. **Ron Butlin,** 'The Story of Our Street', by permission of the author. **Angus Peter Campbell,** 'Gearradh na Monadh a Smeircleit/ Garrynamonie from Smerclate' from *One Road*, Fountain Publishing, Sabhal Mor Ostaig, Isle of Skye, 1994. 'Belly-button' and 'The Dump, Outside Portree, Isle of Skye', by permission of the author. **Kate Clanchy,** 'Hometime' from *Samarkand*, Picador, 1999. **Stewart Conn,** 'Seize the Day' and 'Bedtime Story' from *Stolen Light: Selected Poems*, Bloodaxe Books, 1999. **Joe Corrie,** 'The Image o' God' from *The Image o' God*, Faber & Faber, 1930. **Anna Crowe,** 'Gollop's', first published in *Poetry Scotland*. **Helen B. Cruickshank,** 'There was a Sang' from *Up the Noran Water*, Methuen, 1934. **Des Dillon,** 'Burnt Car', by permission of the author. **Carol Ann Duffy,** 'So Shy' from *Meeting Midnight*, Faber & Faber, 1999. **Alison Fell,** 'Border Raids' from *Kisses for Mayakovsky*, Virago Press, 1984. **Robert Fergusson,** 'The Lee-Rigg' from *The Poems of*

Robert Fergusson, edited by M. P. McDiarmid, Scottish Text Society, 1956. **Anne C. Frater,** 'Caradh/Burying', by permission of the author. **Graham Fulton,** 'The Safeway Mountaineer' from *Knights of the Lower Floors*, Polygon, 1994. **Magi Gibson,** 'a quiet daughter' from *Strange Fish*, Duende Publishing, 1997. **Valerie Gillies,** 'Viking Boy' from *The Ringing Rock*, Scottish Cultural Press, 1995. **Rody Gorman,** 'Gazetteer' and 'Port nan Carbad-Iarainn/Two Trains', by permission of the author. **James Hogg,** 'A Boy's Song', first published in the annual *Remembrance*, London, 1831. Printed in its entirety from a manuscript at Stirling University Library in *James Hogg: Selected Poems and Songs* edited by David Groves, Scottish Academic Press, 1986. **Kathleen Jamie,** 'Lucky Bag' from *Jizzen*, Picador, 1999. **Joyce Johnson,** 'Wee Jamie, a canny young Scot,' from *The Penguin Book of Limericks*, edited by E. O. Parrott, Penguin Books, 1984. **Jackie Kay,** 'Best Pal' from *Three Has Gone*, Blackie Children's Books, 1994. 'Old Tongue', by permission of the author. **David Kinloch,** 'Making Hay' from *Paris-Forfar*, Polygon, 1994. **Helen Lamb,** 'Loch', from *Strange Fish*, Duende Publishing, 1997. **Donovan Leitch,** 'Isle of Islay' from the album *Donovan in Concert*, *1968*. **Tom Leonard,** 'Moral Philosophy' from *Intimate Voices: Selected Work 1965–1983*, Galloping Dog Press, 1984. **Douglas Lipton,** 'A Good Sink: an anecdote', by permission of the author. **Liz Lochhead,** 'View of Scotland/LovePoem' from *Bagpipe Muzak*, Penguin Books, 1991. **Christine De Luca,** 'Lonabrack at Littlure' from *Voes & Sounds: Poems in English & Shetland Dialect*, The Shetland Library, 1995. 'A shuttle o soonds', by permission of the author. **George MacBeth,** 'One Gone, Eight to Go' from *Poems from Oby*, Secker &

Warburg, 1982. **Norman MacCaig,** 'November Night, Edinburgh' from *The Sinai Sort*, The Hogarth Press, 1957. **Hugh MacDiarmid,** 'The Bonnie Broukit Bairn', from *Sangschaw*, 1925. 'The Bubblyjock' from *Penny Wheep*, 1926. **Anne MacLeod,** 'Leaving Stromness' and 'Easter Eggs', by permission of the author. **Kevin MacNeil,** 'The Room', by permission of the author. **Ruaraidh MacThòmais (Derick Thomson)** for 'Lion/Web', by permission of the author. **Brian McCabe,** 'Dumpling' from *Body Parts*, Canongate, 1999. **James McGonigal,** 'Knee-high to a Poem', by permission of the author. **Gordon Meade,** 'A Cormorant in Oils' from *The Scrimshaw Sailor*, Chapman Publishing, 1996. 'The Song of the Grasshopper', first published in *Nomad*. **William Miller,** 'Willie Winkie', first published in 1841. **Edwin Morgan,** 'Midge' and 'Seal' from *Virtual and Other Realities*, Carcanet Press, 1997. **Ken Morrice,** 'Guttersnipe', by permission of the author. **Edwin Muir,** 'Scotland's Winter', from *Collected Poems 1921-1958*, Faber & Faber, 1960. **Charlotte Munro,** 'Scatter-brained Chances' from *The Voice of the Bard: Living Poets & Ancient Tradition in the Highlands & Islands of Scotland*, Canongate, 1999. **Donald S. Murray,** 'An Incomplete History of Rock Music in the Hebrides', by permission of the author. **William Neill,** 'A Celtic History' from *Selected Poems 1969–1992*, Canongate, 1994. **Catriona NicGumaraid (Catriona Montgomery),** 'Rodhag, 2000 A.D./Roag, 2000 A.D.' from *An Aghaidh na Siorraidheachd/In the Face of Eternity*, edited by Christopher Whyte, Polygon, 1991. **Siusaidh NicNeill,** 'Dancing Skies', by permission of the author. **Mark Ogle,** 'Saturday View' from *A Memory of Fields*, Akros Publications, 2000. By permission of the estate of Mark Ogle.

Janet Paisley, 'Sarah: Fed Up', first published by Scottish Book Trust as a National Year of Reading 1998 poem-postcard. 'Sharleen: Ah'm shy', by permission of the author. **Tom Pow,** 'Crabs: Tiree', by permission of the author. **Tessa Ransford,** 'Purity' from *Scottish Selection*, Akros Publications, 1998. Previously published in *Light and Mind*, Ramsay Head Press, 1980. **John Rice,** 'Dazzledance' from *The Dream of Night Fishers: Scottish Islands in Poems & Photographs*, Scottish Cultural Press, 1998. 'Dreamscape at Bedtime' and 'Wee Jenny', by permission of the author. **Robin Robertson,** 'The Royal High School' from *A Painted Field*, Picador, 1997. **Sandy Thomas Ross**, the pen-name of three Ayrshire men, 'Sandy' MacMillan, Thomas Limond and A. L. (Ross) Taylor, for 'Voodoo for Miss Maverick' from *Bairnsangs*, *Nursery Rhymes in Scots*, Alloway Publishing Ltd (originally published by Macmillan, 1955). **Dilys Rose,** 'Performing Doll' from *Beauty is a Dangerous Thing*, Top Copy, 1988. **David Scott,** 'Kite' from *New Writing Scotland 5* edited by Carl MacDougall and Edwin Morgan, Association for Scottish Literary Studies, 1987. **Iain Crichton Smith,** 'River, River', first published by Macdonald Publishers, Midlothian, 1978. **Sydney Goodsir Smith,** 'The Coming of Spring' from *Figs and Thistles*, Oliver & Boyd, 1959. **Charles Hamilton Sorley,** 'When You See Millions of the Mouthless Dead' from *Marlborough and Other Poems*, Cambridge University Press, 1916. **William Soutar,** 'The Tree' from *Collected Poems of William Soutar*, Andrew Dakers Ltd, 1948, with grateful acknowledgement to the Trustees of the National Library of Scotland. **Kenneth C. Steven,** 'Grey Geese' from *The Scots Magazine* (Vol. 149, No. 4, October 1998). **Robert Louis Stevenson,** 'Where Go the

Boats?' and 'Escape at Bedtime' from *A Child's Garden of Verses*, first published 1885, reprinted in the Mainstream Publishing Facsimile Edition, 1990. **Belle Stewart,** 'The Berryfields o' Blair' from *Till Doomsday in the Afternoon: The folklore of a family of Scots Travellers, the Stewarts of Blairgowrie* by Ewan MacColl and Peggy Seeger, Manchester University Press, 1986. **Robert Tennant,** 'Wee Davie Daylicht' from *Wayside Musings*, 1874. **Valerie Thornton,** 'The Cat's Tale', by permission of the author. Previously published in *Catacoustics*, Mariscat Press, 2000. **Christopher Whyte,** 'An Daolag Shionach/The Chinese Beetle', by permission of the author. **John Whitworth,** 'Do-it-Yourself Nature Poem' from *The Complete Poetical Works of Phoebe Flood*, Hodder Children's Books, 1997. **Duncan Williamson,** 'Three Riddles' from *The Voice of the Bard: Living Poets & Ancient Tradition in the Highlands & Islands of Scotland*, Canongate, 1999. **Robin Williamson,** 'the lady with the book' from the CD *Ring Dance*, Pig's Whisker Music, 1998. **Douglas Young,** 'Last Lauch' from *A Braid of Thistles* published by Wm MacLellan, 1947. **A St Kilda Lament,** from *St Kilda: Island on the Edge of the World* by Charles Maclean, first published in 1972 by Tom Stacey Ltd. Reprinted by Canongate Books Ltd as a Canongate Classic (with new Afterword) in 1996. **The Great Silkie of Sule Skerry,** Child 113 (*Proceedings, Society of Antiquaries of Scotland*, 1852.). **The Wren and the Robin,** from *Popular Rhymes of Scotland*, W. & R. Chambers, 1870.